Nothing is about 'us.'

"He is the artist; we are merely his instruments."

To Janis Marie Amann and William Haven Pollock; rest in peace, Mom and Dad.

David Pollock

Art and Poetry by Pollock

Find beauty within and
you have found
beauty everywhere

AUSTIN MACAULEY PUBLISHERS™

LONDON • CAMBRIDGE • NEW YORK • SHARJAH

Ordering Information
Quantity sales: Special discounts are available on quantity purchases by corporations, associations, and others. For details, contact the publisher at the address below.

Publisher's Cataloging-in-Publication data
Pollock, David
Art and Poetry by Pollock

ISBN 9781638295327 (Paperback)
ISBN 9781638295334 (Hardback)
ISBN 9781638295341 (ePub e-book)

Library of Congress Control Number: 2023910249

www.austinmacauley.com/us

First Published 2024
Austin Macauley Publishers LLC
40 Wall Street, 33rd Floor, Suite 3302
New York, NY 10005
USA

mail-usa@austinmacauley.com
+1 (646) 5125767

Thank God for the strength, wisdom, and ability to share,
care, and love.

'Smooth sailing' first rough draft but I had to share... I was in tears writing this one multiple times...

Warm sun so full of life,

Blue jeans, blue eyes, blue skies, blue oyster cult playing over the radio waves...

Smooth sailing,

Smooth sailing...

Countless stars flood the night;

Gentle breeze, dancing, laughing, loving;

Leather jacket, parachute pants, boom box with a cassette and long feathered hair;

Friday night spinning the 33 vinyl playing truth or dare...

Blending in, part of the herd, skim boarding, sunbathing...even good grades...

Smooth sailing...

Lost, shattered, torn, thrashed, mangled, turmoil crashes upon life's shores; unforeseen, unexpected, an unwelcome loss that nobody prepared us for.

This was not in any textbook at school...

More important information than reading and writing

I before e except after C, isn't that the rule?

F the arithmetic and spelling bee...

All fine and dandy when it's smooth sailing...

When it's smooth sailing...

Most unfortunate the path which followed for most...

Most unfortunate…

Earthquake after earthquake, tsunami after tsunami, floods,
fire, disaster after disaster; no smooth sailing,

Darkness fills the skies, gentle breeze turns to category 5,

No more sun year after year an inferno of chaos fuels itself,

Chaos in charge is the way of life; not just alive…

My normal is not yours as yours is not mine…

Most of you know exactly how this feels, your level of
understanding deepens as layers of scars overlap in your
own mind days take a year, years take a day…

Time passes… Tick tock…

Standing still, motionless… Frozen… Stuck in another trap;

No more smooth sailing

Tick tock…

Tingling chill runs down the spine, an energy from within
ignites,

Lightning and thunder; erupting volcano, forces intertwine

Unstoppable force which pinnacles the fight,

Wait, wait, wait…hold on…the fight?

Remember the past, take it back.

tick tock…

That's it…a little further, remember the past…take it
back…

Tick tock…

Remember smooth sailing?

Smooth sailing.

Warm sun so full of life,

Blue jeans, blue eyes, blue skies, blue oyster cult playing
over the radio waves…smooth sailing,

Tick tock…

Smooth sailing…

Countless stars flood the night; Gentle breeze, dancing, laughing, loving;

Leather jacket, parachute pants, boom box with a cassette and long feathered hair;

Friday night spinning the 33 vinyl playing truth or dare tick tock…

Blending in, part of the herd, skim

Boarding, sun bathing, even good grades…good grades…

smooth sailing…

Tick tock,

Once again…

Smooth sailing…

David Heath Pollock – 2018

Good morning, good afternoon and good evening, my name is David Pollock

I am a father, a veteran, a brother and yes a drug addict and alcoholic.

For me, life became quite unmanageable, most of you know what I mean, merely existing from high to high only to reach an all-time low. Loss of jobs, cars, self-respect, and worst of all friends and family.

Bound by invisible restraints of evil…

My thoughts…

A nightmare or a dream???

Confused and lost within myself a labyrinth of chaos, dead end after dead end was my life engulfed by a blaze of drugs and lies…frustrated and mean.

My anger and sorrow fueled by poison into the abyss I plunged further and further, I couldn't stay clean. Clutching the very substances that were killing me, delusional thoughts of my life's final scene. wait, wait, wait…hold on… My life's final scene…

Wake up, Daddy, wake up!!! Wake up, Daddy, please we plea! Wake up, David, wake up, bro! All so desperate to save my life; help me save me from…me?

Wake up, Daddy, wake up!!!

How refreshing a ride to white city in a van labelled DAV.

Where am I? The source VA rehab facility. They kept me busy with a job doing intensive therapy, gave me a little responsibility, made me feel life family and put me in a class called SATP.

By now the fog has lifted, able to see life's beauty; I have clean pee

Introduced to mindful action, self-acceptance and other helpful groups such as CIP. Diagnosed with and treating PTSD. No longer a martyr nor opposer of society. Shown a new way to live, basically a new identity.

Overflowing with happiness and building on integrity; growing stronger day by day all aspects of life even experiencing feelings of humility.

Thanks to a group of strangers showing me how to love and trust again…

Reminding me what it is to be family.

My love goes out to all…

Especially those working via anonymity.

all of this and more for me?

Today victory is yours and mine, ours.

Victory is ours today!!

Hooray, hip hip hooray!!! God bless us all today!!! We need a chair in a meeting, not a eulogy.

This is just a small fraction of my story…

Now you know a little more about me…

There is much more and for those of you who care…

Just love me…

David Heath Pollock – 2015

I want to know your soul…
Your true being your experiences,
Pleasures, heartache, misery, and all the pain.
I want to know your soul;
I yearn to feel your soul fall in love with mine,
Yours and mine;
Spiritual presence touching, caressing,
Dancing, nourishing…
Plenty, abundant, limitless, and bountiful
I want to know your soul…
I yearn to feel my soul and yours intertwine, the soul cannot
be seen and is blind
Yet it sees and feels everything;
The soul is universal, uncontroversial,
Uncommercial, absolute without rehearsal.
I want to know your soul,
Neither man nor woman; both man and woman
Plenty, abundant, bountiful always strong; never weak.
Energy, presence, pure and divine invisible but seen, blind
but can see
our core of existence,
Our true being.
I want to know…
I want to know your soul…
Love, love is…to know your soul…

David Heath Pollock – 2018

Pollock
2018

Not sure how much longer I can read some of these posts. People complaining that have little to nothing to complain about…big house, nice car, everything they ever wanted even a poolside bar…but the moment something does not go their way…oh pooh I broke a nail…the repair man left footprints on my carpet… I got a paper cut; it better not to leave a scar. Your issues are valid; yes, but please put into perspective of what is going on in the world today…people are starving in the streets…for real…people are dying every day of starvation in the streets…think about this next time you decide to call the police. Should I complain about homeless people living under the bridge or in a tent…not my problem nor my fault when a bulldozer wipes the area clean.

Someone's entire life is placed into a dump truck and hauled away as the diesel engines spew black smoke clouding their judgement, masking the truth

Leaving them with nothing not even a change of clothes or their last bid of change. Thirty-five cents… How on earth does this make any sense? How could stealing someone's last 35 cents make sense? To me, it is nonsense; reeking of injustice is the only scent.

In perspective, you drive up your street to an empty lot where your house and all of your belongings used to be… Now imagine; no insurance I guess now you're free… oh and that car you're driving… Yep, got stolen as you wept on the empty lot while down on your knees. Ask God why he did such a thing or how he allowed this to happen to you… At the mercy of another human yet again abused, Frustrated and confused… You realize that your cellphone was in the car…nowhere to turn… No friends, no family…certain there is a lesson to learn… By the way, your ride is here; the good old boys in blue were nice enough to offer a ride to the country line… For free!!!

I might as well be screaming at the top of my lungs!!!

Yada, yada, yada…blahhh, blahhh, blahhh…as by now most have heard more than enough of my world too much truth to be told and have scrolled to the funny meme where they will lol… Because it is much less painful to laugh than cry…or place yourself in another's shoes… Well, probably bare feet in this case. If you are still reading and perhaps a tear is running down your cheek just as mine while I type away…while I pray…I type and pray, may these words catch the eye of someone who cares. Someone who really gives a shit and has the means or dares to make an effort, make a difference, anyone, anything…even just a hello with a smile to the person in need may save their life…believe me I know… I have been amidst the wildlife… I do not care if you have rubbed shoulders and stood tall with the wealthy; I want to know if you have sat on the ground with the sick and unhealthy; someone in need and talked with them like they were a human being or even broke bread with them breathlessly… This is impressive and takes more heart, gut and soul…empathy… If you have ever been down to your last dollar, you can probably relate to my point…

I have a warm dry place to lay my head, max (my friend, dog) and I have food and water, electricity, my basic needs are met. I have an amazing spiritual connection with (none of your business) I am blessed! There are literally billions of people less fortunate than myself and would trade places with me in a heartbeat…

How may I help you???

I love you!!!

I can only guess that these people know adversity

'now' how horrible is your life

and

What were you complaining?

About?

David Heath Pollock – 2017

"God's Glue"
Pollock
2018

Pollock
2018

I am...

The warmth of the sun on a cold day, the moisture of water
to quench your thirst,
That cool spot in the shade on a hot day;
The one your reach for when life is at its worst...

I am...

The same wind that you flew your kite in as a child,
The waves you played in at the beach,
Every creature tame and wild,
My lessons are taught not only by those who preach

I am...

The tears you shed in laughter and sorrow,
The mountains and valleys for all to see,
Complete with you bringing another day tomorrow,
Witness to your every sense and urge
Together no matter the situation we are free...

I am…

You feel me and you know me…
You see me and you show me…
You know who I am…
I need no introduction because

I am…
"You can't take my happiness away no matter what you do;
only I have that power."

David Heath Pollock – 2016

Pollock
2018

Pollock
2018

Alone…

Are we ever really without another…

Still is the air quiet can be heard

You all I consider sister and brother,

Clouds far above, birds' eye view of Earth;

Our mother…

Alone…

The whispers in the wind…

Thoughts of mind,

Always knowing who, what, where, when and why

Destination already known

relax and unwind,

Path is uncertain; everchanging, blind…

Destiny unchanged by our kind…

Alone…

Never am I, never are you

Never are we…

Alone…

Even when standing by ourselves…

alone…

Just write, it's right…

Aren't there rules?

Sure there are rules…

The first rule is that there are no rules…

Just write…just right…

I hope my words are not heard but felt,

Like making love on a pool table felt,

Not really…FELT,

Some languages from the left to the right

Others have some different rules

Top to bottom or bottom to top

Letters or characters?

Who cares…

Just write

Whatever you write is right;

Remember the rules?

THERE ARE NO RULES…

David Heath Pollock – 2019

"Apple of My Eye"
David Pollock
2018

Pollock
2018

This is Max whom I rescued at six weeks old from a van in Ashland, Oregon… He has played on the beach, ran in the redwoods, climbed mountains, gone crazy in corn fields, stayed in the finest hotels, flown in a seat on four commercial airlines, met hundreds of veterans at the V.A. Hospital, swam in rivers, played in the high plains, danced in the desert enjoyed an ice cream at Baskin Robbins,

enjoyed many a sunrise as well as sunset, been silly in the snow, traveled across the country and much, much more…

"I rescued him one day, he unconditionally rescues me every day…"

I love you, Max!!!

Old and tired…driven into the ground, no more tires, temporarily retired, old and tired without tires,
Still willing, strong-hearted and full of steel
Strong chassis full of will

old and tired…
Willing to go wheeling,
Just needs a wheel and your strong will
old and tired…
Driven into the ground; no more tires temporarily retired, just like us after a long life; long day, sunsets, old and tired…
Needs a break, well-deserved rest…
Eventually, she sheds her wheels and demands a break, well-deserved rest; old and tired…
She is willing if you're willing to invest…love, patience, understanding and skill oh man to drive her again…
I can visualize the very moment… What a thrill!!!
Only one crew worthy to perform such justice; they'll revive her from the dead, replace her heart and get her on the road again,
Dress her up head to toe,
Shiny rims, fat tires, clean lines and roll bars
Guaranteed to impress with her new look and if she's lucky she will make his personal collection
Wait wait wait shaking my head…

I am just a passerby, an artist and a dreamer…she is not
even mine but I am a visionary just like you and you, old
and tired…

David Heath Pollock – 2018

First rough draft… Ten minutes creative writing but life is
happening. Max had to potty now, time to run… Will
lengthen and revise.
Leaves change color from green to yellow, perhaps a shade
of purple or red then finally brown
Finally freedom is near as tether withers away,
Limb holds tightly with all its might, sucking every ounce
of energy possible through darkness and light.
Aided to freedom by wind snapping the worn-out tether old
and tired
Limb falling dormant has no choice but to release its grasp
Once mighty and powerful which stood up to every gentle
breeze as well as a category five finally free to dance in the
wind
Finally weightless, twisting and turning,
No destination just flying free; effortlessly
Not falling…dancing …
Leaves leaving
Its only home ever known
Dancing not crying
Dancing in the wind
Dancing to the ground;
Life sucked from them yet full of life dancing in the wind
A silence louder than the chaos of war
A stillness busier than a colony

A single teardrop, last breath of life runs down cheek.

Leaving a river of memories in its path all the laughter, sorrow, love and pain;

Every door ever opened; every heart ever broken…

A single teardrop containing life's vast ocean…

Every smell; every scent,

Every dollar; every cent,

Every letter written; every letter sent

From birth to death

Everything between in every sense…

Reality and fantasy here is where they finally meet… intertwine

Mine is not yours as yours is not mine where one finally learns the true meaning of life

All the answers right here at this very moment

How ironic the meaning of life

How ironic the meaning of life…

Where all the answers to life are so clear, so vivid…so alive

How ironic, life's answer is death

So few ever experience true freedom in the physical vessel we call life.

Most are trapped in a prison cell searching

Always searching for something, someone and somewhere…

True freedom for most come only after the beautiful dance of death

The beautiful dance of death…

Spirit finally uncaged by death

David Heath Pollock – 2021

Just breathe…

Forget your bills and all your worries…

Just breathe…

End the rush rush and hurry hurry

Just breathe…

Life is much more than scamper and scurry…

Just breathe…

Moving too fast; things get blurry…

Just breathe…

Slow life down…

And just…

Breathe…breathe…

David Heath Pollock – 2018

Rough draft like life: unrefined, raw, natural
'My perspective'
Beauty is natural…
Throw out all your makeup and just be the perfectly
beautiful person you are…
Man, woman, child, dishwasher, athlete, or even admiral;
Embrace acceptance and throw out all the hype of how we
must look like someone or something that we are not
This concept to me seems ludicrous, quite bizarre
The rewards are endless perfection cannot be obtained until
you understand that imperfect is perfect; not everything is
meant to be bilateral,
Save money, save time, even take a load off your mind;
Feel better, save resources… And so much more…
"You are beautiful; stop hiding!"
Wipe away the mask of imperfection and
Wipe away the mask of imperfection and lies,
Honorable judge 'Jehovah' presiding;
Drop the façade, just be yourself…open 'your' eyes;
If others cannot or will not accept you for you,
Wouldn't you like to know???
A beautiful woman, a child of God (you know who you are)
looked into my eyes after 10 long years of distance, absence
and silence and simply said, "The past is the past."
For this I am grateful,

More alive, once again loving myself enough to care; not only about self but others now there's a paradigm shift of contrast…

I can honestly look in the mirror today and be OK with who I am.

Believe me this has not always been the case and time shall divulge the answers at last.

For closure, I will say to those who care;

Thank you, and for those who may be hurting, even in despair;

Never give up hope, never lose faith, and hold on tightly with all your might and strength…

When time is lost and lights are dim, just hold on to anything…

Anything…be it a childhood memory, a good grade in school, taste of favorite flavor of ice cream,

Feel the victory of first solo tying of a shoestring…

Anything…

And reach…reach out with the last ounce of being left and take a leap of faith not only in Him but in another…

Take a leap of faith in the right direction…

Soon in the mirror you will awaken to a positive reflection.

Familiar emotions shall emerge from dark to light,

Just as day shall break to night

Feel the warmth of sun in early morn upon your skin

Yet once again life is full of sisters and brothers…

In the mirror, embrace your true reflection.

This is just…

Well, this is just

'my perspective.'

David Heath Pollock – 2018

All the battles ever lost
All the battles ever won
All the souls drifting at sea,
Lost
All the battles ever won
All the battles ever lost
All the souls which have navigated home
All the defeat
All the victory
All the pain, agony, starvation, despair lack of relief
Defeat
All the victory
All the defeat
All the honor, courage commitment
Abundance of love
Victory
All the battles ever won
All the battles ever lost
Predetermined
The war has already been won…
'His' war has already been won…
"Today I have less possessions than yesterday, however, I possess much more than ever."

David Heath Pollock – 2022

"You are the sky, never-ending, limitless and vast…beauty admired, adorned, endless…future, present, and past…you are life and death, light and dark, sun and moon, up as well as down and all around…you are scorching hot yet ice-cold; wet yet dry; invisible but seen…
You are everything while you are nothing…

David Heath Pollock – 2020

Pollock 17

Pollock 12

Airman Pollock reporting for duty, sir and ma'am…

All chronometers have been checked, all personnel are accounted for…

Birds are prepped and over fire.

Pies have been tasted, I am no liar

Bold pot of coffee has been brewed,

Sweet potatoes and tasty buns of course not having them would be rather rude,

Green beans saturated in mushroom soup and those tasty fried onions (added a pinch of cayenne for some attitude), fresh cranberries with secrets being brewed,

Stuffing with herbs and spices causing taste buds to protrude.

From my table to yours on this special occasion known as Thanksgiving,

Please recognize where credit is due,

May God always comfort your mind, body and soul.

Blessings from me to you.

"Ironically, the most beautiful place on the planet is the same as the ugliest place on the planet, inside of one's own mind."

David Heath Pollock – 2022

JOY PEACE HOPE

Who are you???
No, no, no…
Not who you tell people you are; not your smoke and
mirrors;
Not who others think you are…
Not who you want to be,
But simply…
Who are you???

No, no, no

Not where you work;
Not what you do;
Not on the surface;

JUST ASKING YOU TO BE TRUE.

Who are you???
What are your dreams? What do you want to do?
Perhaps this is you?

Why me???

As a child all seemed normal until Mom died,
Eleven years old scared and confused,
Feeling alone and empty inside,
Emotionally numb mentally abused…
Why me???
Isolation sets in; days are dark,
Few friends left; I didn't care,
Neither here nor there,
Now I am twelve, a year has passed; no walk in the park,
Numbing the pain hiding the scars, alcohol and drugs what
an affair…

Why me???

Things in past I had taken for granted were
Lost one by one,
Home from school nothing to eat,
Cupboards bare…
Homework to do, head to my room, flick the switch only to
see darkness…
Now I am scared…
Thirteen and high without an adult, no food, no power no
water to take a shower,

No clean clothes for school,
In my bed crying as I lay…

Why me???

Where is everyone???
Where have they gone???
Friends, family, hello, hello, anyone!!!
Help, help I cry and scream…
Why me???
What did I do wrong to deserve this???
I did my homework…
What did I miss???
I cleaned my room,
Where were you???

Why me???

Scars so deep reach the soul,

All along I thought I was alone…
How wrong I was, now I know,
He kept me safe,
He got me through,
Yes, I strayed my path will prove.

I am strong, I made it through…
I thank God it was me, and none of you.

This is why me!

David Heath Pollock – 2019

'Emotion'

Here are two photos taken just hours apart of the ocean;

Turbulence, force and power to respect portrayed in one;

Serenity, peace and tranquility in the other;

Opposite ends of the spectrum although both are still in motion;

While kind, caring, and loving is our mother; she is capable of crashing and smashing with forces beyond belief,

Deserving of our attention and devotion, as I create my art I hear her roar,

Waves force thrusting, pounding, and shaking the shore;

Over and over her violent cry to us one after another,

I pray her words are not falling upon deaf ears of those in power, reduce one's footprint, dilute the toxic

Poisons, abolish the smother…

This is 'our earth; our mother.'

Take a moment to see the beauty, admire her grace, her laws of existence;

It's not too late to save her through perseverance, persistence and resistance…

Love her emotion

Feel the pulse of her motion

Protect Mother Earth and her ocean;

Care, concern, observance and love…

Crying for her I am as I write…

Praying, we all take action which starts with an emotion…

Starts with an emotion…

Emotion…

David Heath Pollock – 2018

Crime on crime, scars upon scars overlapping, intertwining, understanding deepens, analyzing your own scars of body and mind.

Years upon years of trauma
beach glass repeatedly slammed upon the shores rounded and dull yet remains beautiful as ever perhaps more so.
Powerful swells surge;
agitated and raging oceans gaining momentum and strength from each gust of wind, tropical storm and hurricane combining their powers to form an impressive amount of energy able to devour anyone and anything in its path…unstoppable forces to cleanse the earth of its unwanted debris…
Yet we are still here, you and I
Will stronger than any storm we stand the test of time,
True to our form time after time we tell the tale of our endless nights of silent cry.
Yes, tears flow down our cheek from the eye.
Year after year
Never running dry…
Never running dry…
Forever a teardrop releasing our pain from corner of our eye…
I love you all,
until the day I die.

David Heath Pollock – 2020

My reality is not yours as yours is not mine.
Neither his, hers, nor theirs
always his, hers, and theirs…
sometimes ours while running parallel; shared.
Still unique only mine; not yours, not even mine. Owned
but not owned; never purchased, always earned.
sometimes… Forever yours and mine.
Always never everyone's but all mine, his and hers at the
same time.
There is no time.
forever.

David Heath Pollock – 2017

Took two minutes to write…a lifetime to live but only two minutes to write…

I was in the middle of billions of people, a grain of sand on the beach, anxiety was winning the battle, bullets of sweat flying in every direction…

Taking aim at whoever happened to be in the line of fire
Casualties lay dead in the streets
Twisting and turning I lost
my sense of direction…
I must reach safety soon…
Soon I must reach safety…air…
Gasping for air as my airway tightens more bullets fly…
Blurring my vision spinning in circles not only in my mind…
I close my eyes
darkness covers light…
Spiraling into the darkness…
Twirling…twirling…twirling turns to dance; in the darkness
Dancing toward the light
Once again able to breathe; tense muscles loosen their grasp releasing my soul
Dancing in a storm of people from darkness to light…
Dancing from darkness to light
No more bullets being fired
No new casualties lying in the street
Ahhh, safety in a crowd of billions

eyes open now dancing in a crowd of billions…

Dancing in a crowd of billions in the streets.

David Heath Pollock – 2020

Gentle touch,

Soft glow,

Early morn she will rise,

Kisses head to toe,

Lust, friction, passion; everlasting passion

Passion filling loin,

Again and again,

Thrusting rhythm

Sweat, heat, friction, action;

Burning desire

wave after wave, contraction after contraction
uncontrollable satisfaction…

Over and over; again and again;

Yes…

David Heath Pollock – 2018

Another life has been saved today,

MIRACLES HAPPEN ALL DAY, EVERY DAY!

To some a father a brother, sister, or mother; your niece or nephew, perhaps even your grandmother or grandfather…

Another life has been saved today!!!

MIRACLES HAPPEN ALL DAY EVERY DAY!!!

A dishwasher, CEO, veteran, carpenter…

What's the difference?

Another life was saved today!!!

Peace be with you!

May someone you know; perhaps the person in the mirror be touched by his presence, his power, his unconditional love…

Another life has been saved!!!

MIRACLES HAPPEN ALL DAY, EVERY DAY!!!

David Heath Pollock – 2021

Seventy seconds of uninhabited writing…no rules just pen to paper…there is no such thing… Just write… Yadda, yaddda, yadda, blah, blah, blah… My reality is not yours as yours is not mine, neither is nor hers but theirs, never theirs and always his and hers. My words are for me; they are mine. I do not own them, neither do you, but they are seen, heard and felt, meant to be felt… No really felt like making love on the felt of a pool table, REALLY FELT, not just felt by the felt but feelings of passion not just the 8 ball but all… The cue ball smashes, kisses, and caresses all the balls into the hole skipping across the felt as it is FELT…

David Heath Pollock – 2020

Just breathe…

Forget your bills and all your worries

Just breathe…

End the rush and hurry…

Just breathe

Life is much more than the scamper and scurry…

Just breathe…

Moving too fast things get blurry…

Just breath…

Slow life down

And just…

Breathe…

"Love others more than you love yourself."

David Heath Pollock – 2022

This man will support whoever is put in office!!!

This man will have honor, courage and commitment in everyday life!!!

This man will help anyone he can whenever he can!!!

This man shall show respect to his commander-in-chief even if he does not agree with him or her!!!

This man would die for his country and fellow man if need be!!!

This man took oath to uphold the Constitution of the United States.

I have PTSD.

I do not want friends; I need them…

To need something or someone you do not want…

We have all seen this darkness somewhere in our lives;

A beautiful rose proudly displays its thorns just close enough to protect itself;

Yet distant from its own touch,

Like a shadow with no light,

We cannot see it, but it can be visualized,

Present while absent,

Lust or love?

A one-way street,

"THE SOLUTION LIES WITHIN EVERY PROBLEM."

Blind to reality,

Fantasy appears much more vividly…

Every solution lies within,

Guess what this implies?

The one common denominator in all the lies,

The deception,

The deceit…

I have PTSD I do not want friends; I need them,

Do they need me?

Am I the solution to the problem?

Am I the problem hiding the solution within?

Who is the beautiful rose?

Who is the thorn?

Wait…

Perhaps we are all both from the day we are born…

Halo with forked tail and horn…

Calm in the eye of the storm…

David Heath Pollock – 2021

You earned it…he gave you the strength,
Courage and wisdom, the 'serenity'
Overcame the insanity…
You are blessed to have been touched by him…
"Approval from others is nice, not necessary."

David Heath Pollock – 2022

What we focus on is how we see the world…

The broad overview would be how one sees the world as they rush, hurry and chase monetary gain… The mid view is slowing life down a little and taking notice as you walk through life, the close up, really connecting with nature is actually stopping to appreciate the beauty which is so abundant all around on a daily basis. Unfortunately, few feel they have the time to appreciate or they just forget. Take it back in your mind…tick tock…that's it take it back to our youth and remember the past…tick tock…remember lying in a field of grass watching the clouds drift by so effortlessly without a care in the world… Watching the trees dance in the gusts of wind. Remember playing tag until you were called inside by your folks? Tick tock…remember the past take it back to how simple life really is…and should be…still yesterday is here but gone, tomorrow is not yet and may never be…

Cherish what is… Today here and now…tick tock… Breathe in unison with the universal pulse…

David Heath Pollock – 2020

"We as a species in general tend to value materialistic items more than we value a life of a human and especially much more than the life of another species. It is rather disheartening and shows yet once again vanity of the *Homo sapien* will kill planet earth."

David Heath Pollock – 2022

"We are a very vain and destructive species; quite unfortunate as we are supposed to be the most intelligent, yet we allow our vanity to overshadow our intellect."

David Heath Pollock – 2022

"Soaring like an eagle while living in a tent."

David Heath Pollock – 2019

"One person without money may add more value to life than an army with all the money in the world."

David Heath Pollock – 2022

"Find beauty within and you have found beauty everywhere."

David Heath Pollock – 2022

"Too blessed to be stressed."

David Heath Pollock – 2022

"More willing and capable to enjoy life and love others while remaining less willing to take crap. This to me is success."

David Heath Pollock – 2022

"Save our mother earth, save the ocean."

David Heath Pollock – 2018